SpringerBriefs in Economics

More information about this series at http://www.springer.com/series/8876

Friedrich List (1789–1846); oil-painting portrait by his daughter Karoline (named Lina), 1881; original in the possession of Reutlingen University

Eugen Wendler

Friedrich List's Exile in the United States

New Findings

Springer

Eugen Wendler
Reutlingen
Germany

ISSN 2191-5504 ISSN 2191-5512 (electronic)
SpringerBriefs in Economics
ISBN 978-3-319-23641-4 ISBN 978-3-319-23642-1 (eBook)
DOI 10.1007/978-3-319-23642-1

Library of Congress Control Number: 2015949403

Springer Cham Heidelberg New York Dordrecht London

Printed on acid-free paper

Springer International Publishing AG Switzerland is part of Springer Science+Business Media
(www.springer.com)

For my friends
Tom McMahon,
former major of Reading, PA
and
Prof. Dr. Stephan Seiter
Director of the Friedrich List Institute
at Reutlingen University

Preface

Friedrich List was a prophet of the social market economy, national economy and the infant industry theory. My book, *Friedrich List (1789–1846)—A Visionary Economist with Social Responsibility*, Wiesbaden 2014, is a comprehensive biography of his extraordinary vita and the worldwide influence and reception of List's theories as well as their current significance. His basic theory is that of productive powers and the need to protect infant industries until they are mature enough to compete with international products on world markets. List was a liberal and a democrat who promoted an extended representative democracy, including respect for human rights and civil liberties to accompany industrial development.

List's exile in the USA between 1825 and 1832 played a very big role in his biography. I have devoted another book to this part of his vita entitled: *Friedrich List—An Historical Figure and Pioneer in German-American Relations*, Munich 1989.

In the fall of 2014, I had the good fortune to trace List's life and work in Pennsylvania. During this visit, I gathered new impressions of List's life in USA and found interesting, unknown sources. These new findings are collected in this booklet.

In the discussions that took place after the lectures I held during my short stay, I realized that public knowledge about List was very limited; furthermore, there was no awareness of the fact that the emigration survey List took in 1817 marks the beginning of public opinion research.

In 1816/17 Württemberg experienced dearth as had not been known since the Middle Ages. The preceding years had been cold and rainy, which had led to crop failure. Food stocks were exhausted. When, in 1816/17, weather conditions were again unfavorable, the population suffered greatly under the extreme rise in prices. Hunger and misery were widespread and numerous businesses failed. Many people had no other option but to sell everything they owned and emigrate to the United States.

The emigrants assembled at the harbor of Heilbronn in the hope of travelling down the Neckar and Rhine Rivers to a better future. In doing so, they often followed the lure of unscrupulous vendors of "coffin ships," who, en route from Holland to the US, bilked them out of their last bit of savings.

In the second half of April 1817, Friedrich List was ordered by the incumbent Minister of the Interior, Karl v. Kerner, to go to Heilbronn, where a large number of emigrants were waiting to leave the harbor. His task was to find out the reasons for this mass emigration and, if possible, to persuade the emigrants to stay. List interviewed approximately 200 persons. Many of the men were the heads of families; thus, the number of emigrants actually amounted to 600–700 persons. Although List warned the people about the dangers of emigration, he was only able to persuade three families to stay in Europe.

On May 7, List informed the Minister of Interior of the results of his study, stating that the intention to emigrate was due to:

1. Prohibitive requirements; reparations for past wars, exorbitant taxes and tolls, high local and district taxes due to bad financial management and corruption
2. Oppression by local and district civil servants
3. Unnecessary bureaucracy, i.e., exorbitant scrivener fees
4. Lethargy of the judicial system, in particular in the event of bankruptcy and foreclosure sales
5. Oppression by foresters and damage caused by wild game
6. Oppression by lairds.

In addition, List mentioned harvest failure, inflation, lack of work, excessive religious devotion, and blandishment from civil servants who wanted to be rid of undesirable persons or speculate on the cheap purchase of property.

At the end of his report, List made suggestions as to how emigration might be curtailed. Among other things, he recommended that the Consul of Württemberg in Holland should gather information about the "coffin ships" in Holland in order to better inform persons who were planning to emigrate. Furthermore, he proposed reintroducing the waiting period of one year between the date of emigration application and emigration in order to preclude overhasty decisions based on wrong information.

This was indeed the world's first survey of public opinion; we can believe that List conducted it very professionally.

From 1972 until 2004 I was professor for international marketing, consumer behavior, and communication at Reutlingen University. From the beginning, I was interested in the economic theories of Friedrich List. It has always been important for me to shed light on the life and merits of our "genius loci." For my List research of more than 40 years, I was given the state award for homeland research in Baden-Württemberg, as well as the *Bundesverdienstkreuz* and the Medal of Merit of the city of Reutlingen.

In 1992 I founded the "Friedrich List Institute for Historical and Current Economic Studies" at Reutlingen University, which I directed until 2014. My successor is Prof. Dr. Stephan Seiter, who is a professor of the ESB Business School of the university. Together with Prof. Dr. Harald Hagemann from the University of Hohenheim, near Stuttgart, we organized an international conference in honor of List's 225th anniversary in October 2014.

This booklet is in remembrance of Reutlingen's most famous citizen, who is also one of the world's three great economists: Adam Smith (1723–1790), Friedrich List (1789–1846), and Karl Marx (1818–1883).

Reutlingen January 2015

Eugen Wendler

Contents

The loading of a coffin ship for immigrants to US about 1830

The interior of a coffin ship

Chapter 1
Overview of List's Biography and Economic Theory

Abstract List had a very eventful biography. Born in Württemberg, he was a political opponent of the king and his government and was therefore obliged to leave his homeland and to emigrate to US in order to escape political persecution. Between 1825 and 1832, he lived and worked in Pennsylvania, becoming a US citizen in 1830. After Friedrich Wilhelm Steuben in the second half of the 18th century, List was to become the second famous German emigrant to US in the first half of the 19th century.

1.1 Important Details of List's Biography

Friedrich List was born on August 6, 1789 in Reutlingen—the economic center of the Neckar-Alb region, 40 km south of Stuttgart. Reutlingen was a free imperial city until the end of the eighteenth century. Until the boy was 14 years old, he attended the Latin school of his native town. After a less-than-brilliant performance, his parents decided to take the mediocre student out of school and train him in his father's tannery. Unfortunately young Fritz took no liking to the tanning trade. Thus, after completing his apprenticeship, he was sent to the office of a municipal clerk in Blaubeuren near Ulm to learn the profession of a clerk. There he became acquainted with the deplorable state of affairs in the administration of the Kingdom of Württemberg.

On November 1, 1816 King Wilhelm I, the second King of Württemberg, ascended the throne. A short time after completing his emigration survey, List submitted the formal proposal to the Württemberg government to found a department of socio-economics at the University of Tübingen. There the upper and middle ranking civil servants would receive an academic education. Thus, the cornerstone was laid for the first department of economics at a German university, which still exists today. The universitas literarum was then expanded to include political science or political economy in addition to the four existing faculties: theology, philosophy, medicine and jurisprudence. Although List's education was insufficient for

E. Wendler, *Friedrich List's Exile in the United States*,
SpringerBriefs in Economics, DOI 10.1007/978-3-319-23642-1_1

an academic post, the king finally approved and named him one of the first three professors of this department (Fig. 1.1).

In the spring of 1819, the famous annual Easter Fair took place in Frankfurt a. M., drawing numerous merchants from all German territorial states. At this fair List met the representatives of several merchants who complained about the many customs barriers in Germany: They lamented the fact that the sluggish economic development of German trade and industry was taking a beating from inexpensive English and French imports; i.e., from the first fruits of industrialization: mass produced goods. At the request of the merchants, List formulated a petition to the German Assembly of Deputies in Frankfurt, which represented the different political interests of the many territorial states. The petition called for measures that would eliminate trade barriers and found an internal free trade union.

The merchants received List's draft with great enthusiasm, whereupon he spontaneously proposed the founding of a "General German Trade and Commerce Association". It was the first interest group of German merchants and would lend authority of the many independent German states to the demands put forth in the petition. The petition failed to find the acceptance of King Wilhelm I, however, who promptly dismissed List from his professorship in Tübingen. List was then elected counsel, i.e., head of the Trade and Commerce Association, to which he devoted his entire enthusiasm and indefatigable energy. With great zeal, he endeavored to make the necessity of an economic union clear to the German kings and princes, as a prerequisite to the political unification of the disjointed German domains, which

Fig. 1.1 Medaillon of Friedrich List as a young professor of state economics; water color 1818; original in the possession of the author

was finally realized after long political discussions through the founding of "The German Tariff Union" in 1834.

While on his mission for the Trade and Commerce Association, he was elected by the city of Reutlingen to represent its citizenry in the Württemberg Parliament. As a member of parliament, he formulated an anonymous leaflet, the so-called "Reutlingen Petition", in which he harshly criticized the administrative, economic, social and judicial shortcomings in the Kingdom of Württemberg. Once again bowing to the king's pressure, the Parliament of Württemberg expelled List for disrespecting the honor of the government and for violating the law of freedom of the press; furthermore he was sentenced to ten months of confinement and menial labor. The severity of this punishment was not so much in the length of time, but rather the menial labor List was required to do. Such a punishment was regarded as defamatory in those days and ruined all future chances of having a political career (Fig. 1.2).

As soon as List learned of the debilitating sentence, he decided to flee to a neighboring country and plead for exoneration. This flight led him via Alsace to Switzerland, where he was granted a resident permit in Aarau. From there he travelled to Paris and London in the spring of 1824. In Paris he met the Marquis de Lafayette, who invited List to accompany him on his planned trip to North America. In London Friedrich List received his first information about railroads—the new means of transport that would initiate the first industrial revolution.

Trusting in the mercy of the king, he returned voluntarily to Württemberg, where he was immediately arrested and taken to Hohenasperg near Stuttgart to serve his sentence. After six-months of confinement, he was released under the condition that he emigrate to the US.

His exile in America lasted from June 1825 until the summer of 1832. In the New World List accompanied General Lafayette on the last part of his triumphant journey along the Atlantic seaboard. He then purchased a farm near Harrisburg, visited the Rappite colonies in New Harmony and Economy, accepted a job as editor of the "Readinger Adler" in Reading, PA, discovered a major coal deposit and was co-founder of one of the first railroad companies in the US. He also published his first book on economics entitled: "Outlines of American Political Economy" as well as other socio-economic writings.

Fig. 1.2 First long-distance German train "Leipzig-Dresden"; lithography 1837

List became an American citizen in 1830. Nevertheless, he and his family were homesick for Germany. While visiting Europe briefly in 1831, List investigated his options for return. This endeavor was made possible when President Andrew Jackson appointed him as American Consul for the Kingdom of Saxony.

Directly after his return to Germany, List tackled one of his most outstanding literary feats: the publication of a multi-volume socio-economic encyclopedia similar to the great work of the French encyclopedists. Unfortunately, his political past prevented him from appearing as publisher. Thus, it was published under the names of Carl v. Rotteck and Carl T. Welcker, who are irrevocably associated with this important reference work. The name of its real initiator faded into oblivion.

In Leipzig, the capital of Saxony, List's energies were directed toward the creation of a German railroad network. His first project was the Saxon railway between Leipzig and Dresden, which was the first long-distance railroad in Germany. For someone politically persecuted as List was, it must have required extreme effort to convince the politicians, merchants and other citizens of Saxony of the necessity and economic importance of this project. List invested his available funds and the modest income from his journalistic activities in the planning and construction of the Saxon railway. He was counting on the professional and financial promises the railway company had made, which, however, were never fulfilled. Indeed, he even had to fight to receive compensation for his large outlays. Instead of the promised position in the directorship of the railway company, the "foreigner" was given the token amount of 2,000 talers. The only opportunity open to the 48-year old was to try his luck in another European country. France seemed to hold the best prospects; therefore, in October 1837, List went to Paris.

Soon after his arrival, he heard that the Academy of Sciences was having a literary competition. Essays answering two questions were to be submitted by December 31, 1837. A few short weeks before the deadline, List decided to enter and submit essays on both questions. The first essay was entitled "Le Système Naturel d' Économie Politique"—"The Natural System of Political Economy"; the second "Le monde marche"—"The world is changing". Due to the time pressure and his imperfect French, the essays did not win a prize, but they are still considered two of List's most important literary works. List then decided to resume his journalistic work in the French capital.

After a three-year stay in France, List returned to Germany hoping to receive a managerial position with the Thuringian railroad. Unfortunately, his active involvement and commitment to the railroad did not pay off. He did, however, receive an honorary doctorate from the law school of the University of Jena in 1840; some months thereafter, Karl Marx, who was 28 years younger, received his doctorate in philosophy at the same university (Fig. 1.3).

After failing to gain a foothold in Thuringia, Friedrich List moved to Augsburg where he finished his main opus: *Das Nationale System der Politischen Ökonomie—The National System of Political Economy*, published in 1841. As the first German language treatment of the history of socio-economics, this work is one of the classics of world literature.

Fig. 1.3 Locomotive with wagon of the first long-distance railway between Leipzig and Dresden; lithography 1837

Its significance lies in the fact that List recognized the political nature of economics and presented his insights in easily understandable, popular language. The book was a resounding success and has been translated into Hungarian, English, French, Swedish, Russian, Chinese, Japanese, Korean, Finnish, Bulgarian, Rumanian, Italian, Spanish, Portuguese and Bengali. Except for Karl Marx' famous book *Capital*, no other German economist of the nineteenth century could even approach List in international renown and acclaim.

Finally, List's work found recognition in Germany. This recognition came too late, however, to recharge his spent reserves of energy. Nevertheless, he undertook three more important trips to Belgium, Austria-Hungary and England, where he predicted that the days of English economic supremacy were numbered and would be surpassed by the United States. In light of this, he traveled to England to gain support for a German-English alliance that would benefit both economies. His "policy of the future" culminated in a treatise: "On the value of and conditions for an alliance between Great Britain and Germany". Such an alliance would enable Great Britain to defend its economic supremacy. For Germany, which had become an economic unit through the tariff union in 1834, the alliance would promote productivity and transform the country into a political entity.

The failure of this endeavor was a cruel blow to his physical and mental well-being. His financial situation worsened. List was a broken man; his fighting spirit and body succumbed to exhaustion and the many adversities. In his despair, he travelled to Kufstein in November 1846 on his way to South Tyrol, where he hoped to improve his battered health. Due to a storm, he was forced to stop and take a room at an inn in Kufstein. Alone and desperate, he set out on November 30, 1846 on his last walk.

His suicide at the age of 57 marked the tragic end of a difficult life.

1.2 Theoretical Foundation of List's Economic System

During his stay in Reading, List published his first book on economics in 1827 entitled "Outlines of American Political Economy". Because of this work, the famous American economic professor and Nobel Prize winner, Paul A. Samuelson, recommended that the name Friedrich List be added to the list of important American economists.

Increasing world trade disproportionalities, the Euro crisis, international debt problems, global warming and other ecological problems have taught economists that laissez-faire capitalism and global free trade in the classical sense are not able to solve the problems of the new century. For this reason, we are witnessing a growing interest in and a renaissance of List's ideas.

In 1998 Michael Lind published an essay in the journal "The Nation", in which he poses the question: "Marx, Smith—or List?" Lind recalls "that List was a long-neglected figure in economics. In fact, List had more influence on industrialization in Europe and East Asia than either Marx or Smith. If the 19th century saw a debate among Smithians, Listians and Marxists, and the 20th century a debate between Smithians and Marxists, the 21st century should see a debate between Smithians and Listians—that is between those who favour laissez-faire global capitalism now, and those who envision a social market version of global capitalism as the negotiated result of generations of differing national and regional paths to development."

It is impossible to briefly explain List's economic and political theories and their significance today. However, we can categorize his ideas according to five major topics:

- Homeland and humanity
- Through prosperity to freedom
- The changing world
- The policy of the future
- The union of the European continent.

List criticized that Adam Smith only considered the private and the cosmopolitan or world economy, but overlooked national economies. Each country has its own character, its own raw materials, its own productive powers, its own culture and so on. Therefore, it would be wrong to preach free trade for all countries. He believed in individual economic policies and, for the less developed countries, he suggested temporary protectionism.

List considered the social aspects of economic policy to be equally important, for example, the social situation of human capital. He promoted fair salaries, participation of workers in company profit and decision-making processes, social security and so on.

With regard to the second category, List criticized man's greed when it comes to power, influence and wealth. Instead of these typical excesses of capitalism, he proposed a structure of wealth that would provide satisfaction and prosperity for all social classes. It would involve a healthy social balance between rich and poor and between nations. Respect for human rights and democratic institutions played a big role for List. He believed that "no nation ever achieved success as an industrial power without also enjoying a high degree of political freedom."

When List speaks of "the changing world", he of course refers to the technological development of the first industrial revolution, in particular the inventions of the steam engine, steamboat, railway and telegraphy. He expected that international trade, commerce and communication would reach all corners of the world. In this sense, he was a pre-thinker of globalization.

List thought in geopolitical categories. His political and economic visions were part of his "policy of the future", the concept of which shall be outlined here. List considered the three most important factors or forces acting on the world economy to be the growth of population, the increase of capital and the development of productive powers. He regarded England, France and USA and, with some reservations, Germany, which was not yet united, to be the most developed nations at the time. Russia and Spain were of secondary importance (Fig. 1.4).

List believed that the economic and political development in the USA would prod England to further expand her industry, taking the necessary means therefore from the consolidation and expansion of her empire. The greater the colonial population and prosperity in Asia, Africa and Australia, the more food and raw material England could import and the more consumer goods she could export. Thus, her wealth and financial resources would increase, as would her power at sea and on land. An "international freeway" would eventually be built between England and China that would "incorporate everything" to the right and left of it. Gibraltar, Malta, Cyprus, Aden, India, Ceylon, Singapore and Hong Kong were examples of such development.

Fig. 1.4 The three great economic theorists: Adam Smith, Friedrich List and Karl Marx; caricature by Karen Caldicott; in: Lind, M.: Marx, Smith—or List? in: The Nation, October 5, 1998, p. 30

No one could say when this might take place, but one might be so bold as to say that the generation to witness this has already been born. According to List, England would "institutionalize trade all over the globe" and try to impose her language and culture on the colonial population, which was used to hard work and subservience. However, he believed that the Arabs would resist colonization.

At the same time, List foresaw that the English empire would not endure. He was sure that Australia, New Zealand and the colonies on the southern and eastern coasts of Africa would gain political significance and probably become independent, as did the United States of America.

List expected that the United States would develop in the second half of the 19th century to the superpower of the western hemisphere. For the second half of the 20th century, he also predicted the rise "of a new world, a second superpower" in the East, "whose population would greatly exceed that of the New World and would at least attain comparable wealth". List was clearly referring to China. He expected the US-American population to grow from 18 million people to 300 million by the end of the 20th century, a prediction that was absolutely correct.

He was not convinced that Russia should be considered one of the leading industrial nations. Russia's social cohesion, culture, constitution, laws and administration were dependent on a number of underdeveloped nations that had to be held together by Russia's military power. List doubted that Russian politicians would manage to solve the nationality problem. On the other hand, he feared that Russia might dominate the European continent, considering the fact that this colossus would continue its path of nation-building and gain considerable strength. Subjugation would not occur, however, if the nations of central and western Europe were united economically and politically.

List was much more sceptical with regard to the future of the African continent. If the population growth in Africa could not be checked, he believed that Tanger and Fort Ceuta, located directly opposite Gibraltar, "might become important for Europe in the event of an invasion from Morocco". If we think of what is happening today in the Ukraine or on Lampedusa, which is the first destination of African refugees, we can see how well List foresaw the future.

As early as 1818, List developed his vision for Europe: one day, all of Europe would celebrate the implementation of a new trading system. Europe would organize a trade congress that would gradually loosen the ropes and chains that prevented trade. The Europe that was divided into many small fragments and differing interests would be unified to become a unique and growing power. In such a unified and liberalized common economic market, without protectionism and trade-barriers, Germany would become a great commercial link between east and west, and between northern and southern Europe. Under the umbrella of external and internal peace, it would achieve wealth and prosperity.

List was convinced that the Osmanic Empire would collapse very soon and that Italy, France and Russia would try to bring the new countries under their influence and control. At the same time, he doubted that the countries of Latin America would make great economic progress. He believed that their economies would be based on the exploitation of minerals and other natural resources and on agriculture.

According to List, the expressed goal of the trading nations of Europe must be to establish sound, democratic governments in Asia, Africa and Latin America, which would be able to protect their citizens and property. Furthermore, Europe should advocate the right to free trade for all nations, thus enabling all nations to acquire the goods they need at a favorable price and to sell their own goods as profitably as possible.

In the text List submitted for the second Parisian literary competition of 1837, he recommended that France should lead the European coalition due to its material wealth, geographical location and degree of civil and political development. Paris would become the center of European trade and the geopolitical intersection of the orient and occident as well as northern and southern Europe. We can thus conclude that List was a "prophet of the European Union".

List bemoaned the petty jealousies that the various governments displayed towards one another. He claimed that "nothing stands more in the way of civilization and progress than the jealous and envious policies with which the European nations try to thwart each other. If they would only promote free trade and equality before the law in Asia and other parts of the world instead of insisting on the exclusive ownership of colonies and the exclusive rights to trade, all of this petty jealousy would disappear and everyone would profit".

The reader will surely agree that while this idea was visionary, the European Union has still not managed to overcome national malevolence and egoism. The ills of the currency union and the cumbersome bureaucracy of the European Union are rooted in this challenge.

We cannot say that List would have been content with the current state of the EU or the currency union. Indeed, it is doubtful that he would have favored the eastern and southern expansion or the currency union. He claimed that membership in such a union should be voluntary; furthermore, he advocated a union of more or less equal states, i.e., states that had developed and industrialized to approximately the same extent.

Chapter 2
New Findings Regarding List's Exile in United States

Abstract During a visit to US, the author followed List's historical traces and uncovered new and interesting information on this "unknown great American". List discovered extensive coal deposits in the Blue Mountains and, in 1831, built together with his business partner, Dr. Isaac Hiester, one of the first railways not only in US, but in the world. List is to be considered one of the most important economists of the last centuries, ranking together with Adam Smith (1723−1790) and Karl Marx (1818−1883). Like Smith and Marx, he developed his own economic system—one that enjoys international esteem even today.

2.1 Impressions of a Journey to Reading, Pennsylvania

On the occasion of List's 225th anniversary, I was invited to visit Reading, Pennsylvania, the American partner city to Reutlingen. My trip was sponsored by the city of Reutlingen and organized by the former mayor of Reading, Tom McMahon (3). The purpose of the journey was to gain insight into List's five-year's exile and work in Reading between 1826 and 1832, to intensify the partnership between Reutlingen and Reading, to present my new book, *Friedrich List (1789 −1846)—A Visionary Economist with Social Responsibility* and, if possible, to find new sources and photographs for my research. I was accompanied by Donna Blagg, the translator of my book (4).

Former Mayor Tom McMahon gave us a guided tour of the city. He showed us the Lutheran Church, where List's youngest daughter Karoline ("Lina") was baptized. She was a gifted painter and in 1881—35 years after List's death—painted three portraits of her father. She had never been satisfied with the portraits by other artists and wanted to express his alert eyes and facial features. One of these paintings is in the possession of Reutlingen University and has been used for the cover of this booklet. List's oldest children, Emilie and Elise, attended the school in the Lutheran Church of Reading.

E. Wendler, *Friedrich List's Exile in the United States*,
SpringerBriefs in Economics, DOI 10.1007/978-3-319-23642-1_2

Fig. 2.1 The baptistry of the Lutheran Church in Reading, P.A., where List's daughter Karoline (Lina) was baptized

Friedrich List lived for a while near the printing office of the *Readinger Adler*, which was located on the present site of the Central Market on Penn Street, below Fourth. Later he lived on the west side of North Fifth Street, between Court and Washington Streets, in a house owned by Henry Christ, a sheriff of Berks County.

With the help of the Historical Society of Reading, we managed to discover the third local residence of the List family: "Ball's house" on 3rd Street below Callow Hill Street. From an old city map, one can imagine that the Lists must have lived a simple and modest life in what was a very small apartment. Neither the street nor the little house exist today (Fig. 2.1).

On a mountain overlooking Reading there is a "List-Road" with an iron memorial in honor of List.

On the second day of our stay in Reading, we were the guests of the current editor of the "Reading Eagle" (former "Readinger Adler"), where List worked as editor from 1826 until 1832. At the entrance to the main building there is a small plaque with the following text: "Friedrich List: famous national economist, diplomat, railway pioneer and editor of the *Readinger Adler*, lived and worked in Penn Street 351 when he published his *Outlines of American Political Economy*".

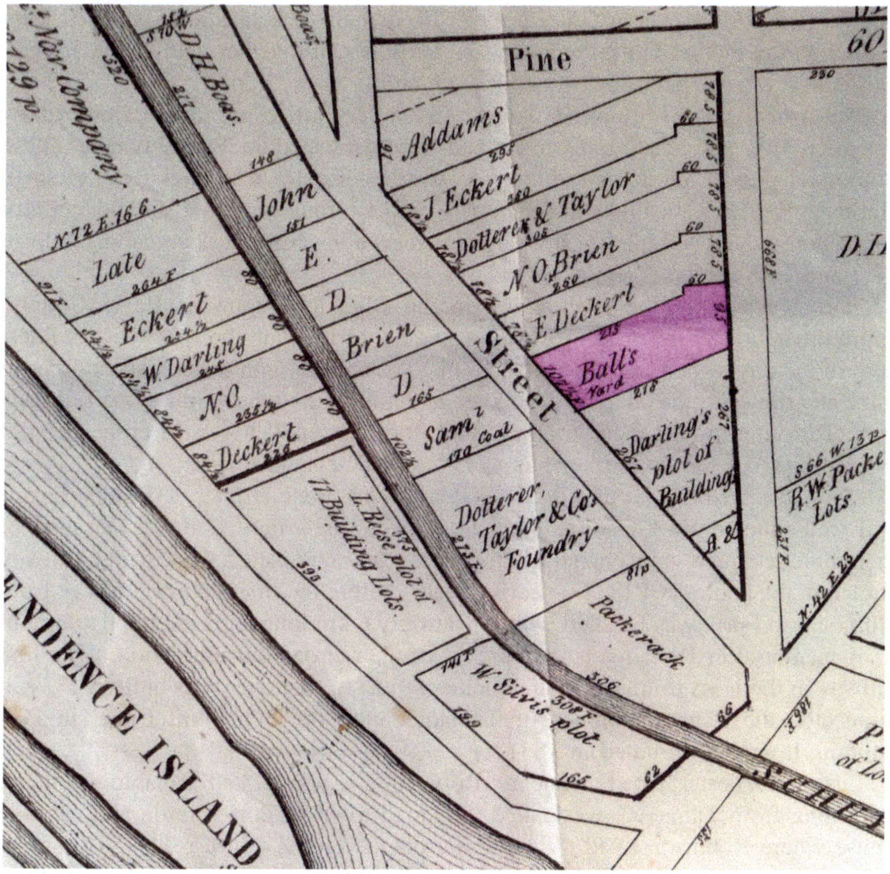

Fig. 2.2 Detailed view of the old city map of Reading, P.A.; original at the Historical Society of Reading

The current owner of the publishing house, Mr. Peter Barbey, is a direct descendant of John Ritter, who engaged List as editor of the German weekly newspaper. The building houses a small museum in which old copies, volumes and photographs of John Ritter and the old printing press, used in List's time, can be seen. The priniting press was the first to be built in Pennsylvania (Fig. 2.2).

A very interesting and impressive experience was our visit to Lancaster County, where many Amish people live. They still cultivate their traditional culture and language; to some extent they live as their ancestors did in the 19th century and speak the typical Pennsylvania Dutch, which is similar to the Swabian dialect. In Kutztown (Kutschastädtle), in the "Katzebuckelweeg", we had a very nice visit with a family and were able to communicate with them in our Swabian dialect.

The Amish have their own newspaper entitled "Hiwwe wie Driwwe", from which a text shall be cited: "Ich will mit die Maem hocke an die Gmee. Ich hock net mit die grosse Meed. Unser Gmee hot vier Bredicher; sie hocke in die Mitt." (I want to sit with my mother in the congregation. I will not sit together with the older girls. Our congregation has four priests; they are sitting in the middle.)

The Amish way of life and language give a very interesting impression of how Friedrich List and his family lived and communicated in Pennsylvania. These impressions were reinforced during a visit to Kutztown University's German Heritage Research Institute and a small outdoor museum with an old country schoolhouse, a stone house of a wealthy farmer, a big barn and two cabins built in 18th and 19th centuries (Fig. 2.3).

During a visit to the coal region in the Blue Mountains of Berks County, approximately 120 miles from Reading, we could imagine the untouched wilderness of the days when List discovered a huge deposit of anthracite coal. In order to mine and transport the coal, he conceived and built one of the world's first railroads from Tamaqua to Port Clinton along the Little Schuylkill River. In order to build the rail bed, the torrential river had to be crossed seventeen times.

List had a business partner in this endeavor: Dr. Isaac Hiester, a medical doctor and well-situated citizen of Reading, lived near List's first residence. In spite of incredible technical and financial difficulties, they completed the 22-mile railway stretch in the autumn of 1831—nearly 4 years before the first German railway from Nürnberg to Fürth was finished, which was only 6 km long and covered flat terrain.

A memorial in Tamaqua is reminiscent of the railroad's inauguration: "The first railway in the USA to transport anthracite with a steam engine was built in 1829; it connected the rich coal mines of Tamaqua with the Schuylkill Canal in Port Clinton. It was inaugurated in 1831."

List and Hiester hired Moncure Robinson, a young and capable engineer. Returning from Tamaqua, we visited the small town of Port Clinton and saw the house where Robinson lived. A memorial plaque on the house reads: "This magnificent 2½ story spacious brick home was constructed as part of a deal made to entice Moncure Robinson, a civil engineer from Virginia, to lay out the proposed railroad from the Schuylkill Water Canal in Port Clinton to the foot of the Broad Mountain (Tamaqua), along the Little Schuylkill River. This house served as his home and office and as a Post Office when he became Port Clinton's first postmaster. It was also used as a grocery store, and has been renovated to the original state."

In a nearby small museum one can find construction drawings, pictures and, of particular interest, instruments and tools that were used to construct the rail bed. We also found a very rare picture of an American train transporting people around 1840. The old rails and coal deposits can still be seen between Tamaqua and Port Clinton. The railroad is out of service today, but there are still large stockpiles of coal along the tracks.

Even today, although the railway stretch is no longer in use and located miles from any industrial centers, one still can imagine the great accomplishment that the construction of the Little Shuylkill railway must have been in the mid-19th century.

Fig. 2.3 Amish people; photograph by E. Wendler, 2014

Its remoteness also suggests how lonely and homesick Karoline List and her children must have felt in the New World. It is therefore understandable that Friedrich List took the first opportunity to move his family back to Europe.

2.2 List's Journey with General Lafayette through the Atlantic Coastal States

2.2.1 Preliminary Remarks

During his journey to Paris and London in April 1824, List became personally acquainted with the famous Marquis de Lafayette. List devoted the first volume of his literary series "Themis" to Lafayette, who expressed benevolent and apprecia-tory words about the author. He praised List for his brave, philosophical mind and the dignity with which he endured his banishment. At the same time, he regretted the tribulations that List suffered, stating that his sympathies and wishes would accompany him to a hopefully brighter future. Lafayette also congratulated him on his command of the French language (Fig. 2.4).

During their first encounter, Lafayette offered to take List with him to North America, whereupon List wrote to his wife, full of enthusiasm: "He has received over 100 letters from persons who want to accompany him and has refused them all. My situation is such that he feels compelled to do everything in his power to help me. When this divine, elderly gentleman embraced me, it moved me to tears. He won't depart until August and will inform us in good time so that we have ample

Fig. 2.4 General Lafayette, lithography of Carl Meyen; original in the possession of the author

time to prepare. Now we need to decide what we would like to do and this can only happen at home."

List's wife was not yet ready to leave Europe. The family thus decided to return to Württemberg. In a letter which Lafayette addressed to List on July 13, 1824, written on board the "Cadmus", he expressed his regret regarding List's decision and his solidarity with him. He affirmed once more that his friends in the US would gladly support a man who believed in the alliance of all friends of liberty.

In January 1825 Lafayette again wrote to List from Richmond (January 21st) and Harrisburg (January 30th), expressing his sincere sympathy and encouraging List to settle in the USA. Hoping he would meet him on June 17th, the 50th anniversary of the Battle of Bunkerhill, Lanayette added: 'If you had come with me, you would have experienced all the amicability the American nation demonstrated to me'.

These letters surely influenced List and his family in their decision to finally emigrate to the United States, albeit with heavy hearts.

When the family arrived in New York in mid-June, List learned of Lafayette's current whereabouts from the Package Boat Line. The general invited him once more to accompany him on the rest of his tour, knowing that List would marvel at the extreme contrast between the old social order in Europe and the superiority of American institutions.

2.2.2 Details of Lafayette's Journey in 1824

In 1824 General Lafayette received a formal invitation from Congress to visit America and sailed on "Cadmus". He was accompanied by his only son George Washington Lafayette. The third member of the party was Auguste Lévasseur, the secretary and historian of the trip. In addition, they had a servant in their delegation (5).

They arrived on Staten Island in July and were guests of Vice-President David Tompkins (1774–1825) on August 15th. During the following journey to Boston, President Monroe introduced the French guests to all ranks of the establishment. They also visited Harvard, heard an address by Congressman Edward Everett (1794–1865) in their honor. They then travelled to Bunker Hill to witness the preparations for the projected monument on August 27th. John Quincy Adams entertained them personally when they travelled to Portsmouth via Lexington, Concorde, Salem, Marblehead and Newburyport. Thereafter, they returned to Boston on September 2nd and left for Hartford, where they were celebrated with great pomp: Lafayette was given a gold medal by the children of the city. Leaving Middletown by ship, they arrived in New York on September 5th. The next day they dined with the Society of Cincinatti, attended a dinner organized by the French citizens of New York and a magnificent fête at the Castle Garden on September 13th. Sailing up the Hudson on the "James Kent" steamboat to Albany, they visited West Point, Catskill, Hudson and Troy, and returned to New York. On September 22nd Lafayette and his delegation left New York for Trenton amidst cannon thunder bidding them farewell. In New Jersey they stopped in Newark, a lovely village located on the banks of the Passaic. They spent the night of September 24th in Newark, continuing on the next day to Princeton, where an honorary diploma was presented to Lafayette. After visiting Trenton, the delegation rode to Bordentown, where they dined with Joseph Buonaparte (1768–1844), Napoleon's brother, who lived there with his son-in-law. The next day they set out for Philadelphia, arriving on September 27th, where practically the entire population welcomed and entertained them for a week. Lafayette was made a member of the Grand Lodge of Free Masons of Pennsylvania and attended a banquet in his honor. Embarking on the Delaware, the party proceeded to Baltimore, visiting Chester and Wilmington en route. They spent four days in Baltimore and arrived in Washington on October 12th by carriage. There they dined with President Monroe and were his guests for several days. With John C. Calhoun (1782–1850), Vice President under John Quincy Adams and Andrew Jackson, the group left Washington on the steamboat "Petersburg", stopping in Yorktown to celebrate the anniversary of the British surrender during the Revolutionary War on October 19th and in Richmond by way of Williamsburg and Norfolk on October 20th. The delegation visited Petersburg on October 31st and moved on to Monticello, where Lafayette was received by his old friend Thomas Jefferson. On the way to Montpellier, they stopped at the University of Virginia in Charlottesville, where they dined with Jefferson and Madison, spent

Fig. 2.5 General Lafayette (1757–1834), "The Hero of the Two Worlds"

four days at Madison's home and finally returned to Washington by way of Fredericksburg on November 21st. They dined again with the President and visited Baltimore as guests of the Agricultural Society, where they met the farmers of Maryland. It was here that a toast was proposed to Lafayette, "the farmer of La Grange". The US Congress received the delegation with military pomp on December 9th. Henry Clay (1777–1852), Secretary of State under John Quincy Adams, introduced the Marquis to Congress, who presented him with a gift of $200,000 and a large tract of land in Louisiana. The group then visited Annapolis on December 16th, returning to Washington by way of Frederickstown, where a public banquet was held in their honor (Fig. 2.5).

2.2.3 *Continuation of the Journey in 1825*

On New Year's day they were given still another dinner by Congress, at which President Monroe was present. They left Washington on February 23rd and travelled to Norfolk, Raleigh and Camden. On March 11th, they were welcomed in Columbia. Great preparations had been made for their entertainment in Charleston, where the delegation arrived on March 15th and was greeted by Colonel Francis K. Huger (1773–1865), whose father had welcomed General Lafayette on his first arrival to America. Leaving by sea on March 17th, Lafayette laid the cornerstone of a monument dedicated to Generals Nathanael Greene (1742–1786), (second most important general after George Washington in the War for Independence) and Kazmierz Pulaski (1745–1779), the founder of the American cavalry at Savannah. They then visited Augusta, Midgeville and Macon, where they met with the Creek Indians. They arrived in Montgomery on April 3rd, in Mobile on April 7th and, after a stormy voyage on the Gulf of Mexico, reached New Orleans on April 8th. There they remained until the 15th, enjoying continuous entertainment and public ceremonies in their honor. Continuing the voyage up the Mississippi, the French delegation arrived in Natchez on April 18th and in St. Louis on April 29th, where they were met by Governor Cole. On May 2nd they arrived in Nashville via the Cumberland River and were welcomed by General Jackson, who presided at a public dinner given for Lafayette and who entertained the delegation the next day at his own home. They continued their journey up the Ohio via the "Mechanic" steamboat, which shipwrecked at midnight on May 8th (Fig. 2.6).

The party was safely taken ashore and continued their journey to Louisville the next day on the "Paragon", which was partly owned by Mr. Robert Neilson, one of Lafayette's party aboard the "Mechanic". After visiting Louisville, Frankfort and Lexington, the party arrived in Cincinatti on May 19th by carriage, having visited Henry Clay at Ashland on the way. After several days of festivities in Cincinatti, they embarked on the "Herald" for Pennsylvania, visiting Uniontown and Elizabethtown en route.

Fig. 2.6 General Lafayette lays the cornerstone of Bunker Hill monument on June 17, 1825 during the celebration of the 50th anniversary of the battle of Bunker Hill

2.2.4 The Journey Accompanied by Friedrich List

Friedrich List and his family had arrived at the harbor of New York on June 9th, 1825. Years later his daughter Emilie recalled their arrival in New York. She was just 6½ years old upon arrival in the New World: "We only stayed there for a few days. Lafayette was there at the time and one of my first recollections is that my father took us children to meet him. The elderly gentleman spoke very kindly and kissed us. Lafayette invited my father to take a journey with him, which my father thankfully accepted as he hoped to make useful acquaintances and, furthermore, to see the country, for he had decided to use the rest of his small savings to buy a farm. He brought us to Philadelphia, rented a small house in the Northern Liberties, a suburb in which mostly Germans lived, enrolled us in an American school and left."

He returned to New York, took a steamship up the Hudson River and met General Lafayette in Albany on July 2nd. The following has been rendered about the meeting in Albany: "At a dinner given to General Lafayette in the Hall of the Capitol, at which Elias Kane presided, there were present as guests, Governor Van Ness, Judge Storey, Mr. Webster of Boston, Judge Woodworth, Judge Spencer, General van Reusselaer and Professor List of the University of Württemberg. Some of the toasts given on the occasion are worthy of being mentioned, for example the one by Professor List from Germany: 'To the United States, which, unlike the ancient republics of the world, creates citizens instead of subjects'."

On leaving Pittsburgh Lafayette stopped at Erie, Buffalo, Niagara Falls, Rochester, Syracuse and Utica, arriving in Albany on June 12th. They returned to Boston on June 15th by way of the Erie Canal and carriage for the fiftieth anniversary of the Battle of Bunker Hill and the laying of the corner stone of the monument on June 17th. Leaving Boston they passed through New Hampshire, visiting Concord and Dover, and arrived in Portland, Maine on June 25th, where they were enthusiastically received. Their journey then took them through Vermont, stopping in Windsor, Woodstock, Montpellier and on to Burlington on June 28th. The group then took the steamer "Phoenix" to Whitehall, from where they continued by carriage to Albany.

Meeting up with the 67-year old general in Albany, List travelled with him and the other two French guests on the remainder of his triumphant tour. For someone who had just arrived, this was an exceptional opportunity to experience life the New World under the most favorable circumstances. The journey lasted 2½ months, during which time List travelled through the most densely populated and most prosperous areas of the country, from northern New York State along the Atlantic seaboard to Maryland and Virginia in the South. Not only was List interested in the social and economic life of his new home, but also in the political and cultural developments as well as the history that had been made on the battlefields of the revolutionary war, where independence had been fought for and the foundation for the new nation laid. List was surely fascinated by the urban centers as well as by the rural farmlands (Fig. 2.7).

While Lafayette and his son George Washington rode in the first two coaches, List normally followed in the third. At times they were accompanied by as many as 2,000 men on horseback to ceremonious receptions. The honor of being a part of this triumphant march must have been a very emotional experience, given the humiliation and grief he had suffered in Europe and during his passage to New World.

On the early morning of July 4th, the 49th anniversary of American independence, Friedrich List and Lafayette returned to New York with the steamer "Chancellor Kent". The party stayed at Bunker's Mansion House on Broadway, an historical building occupied by President George Washington from February 23rd to August 30th, 1790 while New York City was still the nation's capital. It therefore bears the name "the second Presidental Mansion".

When arriving in Manhattan, List experienced an overwhelming welcome for General Lafayette. He saw the people's happiness and joy and was introduced to the most esteemed and influential persons of the country. He then travelled to Pennsylvania via New Jersey, visiting the Brandywine battlefield by way of Chester. Everywhere in Pennsylvania the party was welcomed and cheered, leaving List with the impression that German and French settlers together cheered their French liberator.

On July 20th they visited Germantown and Chesnut Hill near Philadelphia. At Monticello they did what only few others had the honor to do: dine with three men who had been Presidents: Thomas Jefferson, James Madison and James Monroe. On July 25th the delegation again visited Wilmington, Delaware.

Fig. 2.7 Friedrich List, middle aged; original in the possession of the author

The next station was Lancaster, where the entourage was welcomed on July 27th and stayed for three days. The entire population participated in the enthusiastic reception; according to a newspaper there were only a few hands that Lafayette did not shake.

On August 1st they were back in Washington and guests of the President until August 6th. They also visited James Monroe at Oak Hill for several days before returning to Washington. A few days later Lafayette and his entourage visited Culpepper, Faquier and Warrenton before continuing to Monticello, where they were joined by Madison for a visit to Lafayette's old friend, Thomas Jefferson, and escorted by the volunteer cavalry of Virginia. The group returned to Washington on Lafayette's birthday, September 6th, for which the President gave a dinner. Thereafter the four guests left by the steamboat "Mount Vernon" for the mouth of the Potomac, at which point the Frenchmen boarded the "Brandywine" and, with a rainbow stretching across the river, set sail for France on September 8th. They arrived in Le Havre on October 4th, where the Marquis received a warm reception and carried on to La Grange, arriving there on October 9th. The following Sunday a brilliant celebration attended by 4,000 guests was held, a fitting climax to his triumphant tour, which according to Charles Sumner (1811–1874), Senator of Massachusetts, was 'part of the poetry of history'.

While accompanying Lafayette, List met all leading personalities of the United States, including the then incumbent President John Quincy Adams and his successor Andrew Jackson. No German, except the famous General Friedrich Wilhelm Steuben, had as much contact with the important politicians of the United States as List did. For this reason, he was later consulted by members of the Congress regarding matters of European trade.

On September 7, 1825, Lafayette sent List a letter from the "Brandywine", stating that he regretted not being able to support List, who had suffered for his fight for freedom and was thus deserving of recognition by the most important intellectuals and well-meaning persons in Europe. His talent as professor, his commitment to freedom as deputy in the Württemberg Parliament and his prosecution would certainly command the attention and support of many American friends if it weren't for the one indispensable condition that prevailed in this country, namely the need to be able to speak English. Since he was missing precisely this prerequisite, List had no other choice but to become a farmer and learn the language as fast as possible.

The correspondence between Lafayette and List continued even though not many letters remain to document this contact. In November 1826 Lafayette's son George Washington Lafayette wrote that he and his father thought often about the journey with List and wished him the best for his literary endeavors.

In November 1827, List's publication of the *Outlines of American Political Economy* was celebrated by the "Pennsylvania Society for the Encouragement of Manufactures and the Mechanic Arts". President John Quincy Adams attended this festive act, during which Lafayette's role in having introduced List to the United States was mentioned during the toast: "To our guest, Professor List, whose merit has been affirmed by Lafayette's recommendation and by his own credentials with respect to political economy."

On November 28, 1827 List again wrote to his benefactor, the Marquis, in order to inquire into the European market for anthracite coal and the tarrifs that would need to be paid. Unfortunately, we have no knowledge of a response from Lafayette. In fact, only the final sentence of the original letter survives today: "I request, dear General, to assure Mr. George Lafayette and Mr. Levasseur of my high esteem and to accept the assurance of my constant veneration.—Your humble and grateful servant Fréderick List." The letter was found by Mr. J. Bennett Jolan, a local historian of Reading, in a bookshop in Paris. He commented on the letter as follows: "It is a fine example of the ever-active mind of List, making numerous inquiries regarding a number of products, their price, the French duty rate and the possibility of importing them into France." We don't know where the original letter currently is.

2.3 List's Journalistic Support of Andrew Jackson During the Presidental Election of 1828

The political contest between the incumbent President John Quincy Adams and his challenger Andrew Jackson had a long prehistory that culminated in 1824 in their fight for the highest political office of the US. In this election four candidates from the Democrat-Republican party competed against each other. Neither of the candidates won the majority of electoral votes. According to the American Constitution, the House of Representatives must then decide. Although Andrew Jackson had 99 and John Quincy Adams only 84 of the electoral votes (with Crawford and Clay receiving 41 and 37 electoral voltes respectively), the majority of the House voted for Adams, electing him to the sixth president of the United States (Fig. 2.8).

Jackson was deeply disappointed by the decision of the House of Representatives, accusing them of electoral fraud and corruption. In particular, the appointment of Henry Clay as Secretary of State was strongly challenged by Jackson's supporters and led to the split of the hitherto Democratic-Republican Party. The supporters of Adams and Clay then founded the National-Republican

Fig. 2.8 President Andrew Jackson (1829–1837); original in the possession of the author

Party while Jackson's supporters formed the Democratic Party. Consequently, the two parties stood more or less viciously in opposition to each other. The era of good feeling was over; the administration of John Quincy Adams is generally regarded as the era of ill feeling.

Adams and Jackson were two antipodal characters. Adams, proud and reserved, had only a few political friends and a small group of supporters. In many parts of society he was seen as the leader of the aristocratic party. In contrast, Jackson was considered a man of the people who emerged from the underclass. His nickname was 'Old Hickory', because of his involvement in the war against the native Americans. His popularity increased after his defeat in the House of Representatives, since the majority of the population thought the vote was unfair.

Meanwhile, Friedrich List had become the chief editor of the *Readinger Adler* and was thus involved in the election campaign.

List originally supported Adams, who promoted protectionism. John Ritter, who was List's employer, was an avid follower of Jackson. In accordance with the proverb 'He who pays the piper, calls the tone!', List had no choice but serve Jackson. It seems he had no difficultiy switching loyalties, as can be seen in a poem written by List, in which he praises Jackson as a 'hero' (Fig. 2.9).

Indeed, List was very active as a journalist during the presidential campaign of 1828 and championed Jackson's cause so well that Jackson expressed his appreciation for the staunch support he received from the German population of Pennsylvania.

In an article published on December 4, 1827 in the *Readinger Adler*, List wrote: "If we consider the way a man is nominated for public office by virtue of the trust his fellow citizens place in him, then General Jackson will leave Mr. Adams far behind. However, if we consider luck and luck alone, Jackson cannot make the

Fig. 2.9 John Ritter, owner of the *Readinger Adler*; original in the museum of the *Reading Eagle*

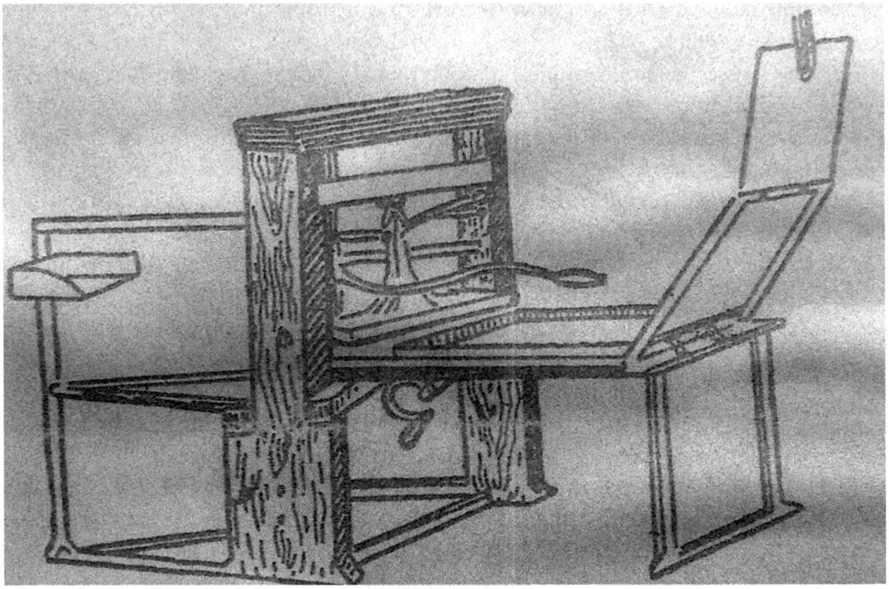

Fig. 2.10 Printing press on which the first *Adlers* were produced; the ancient press was built in a blacksmith shop in Limekiln in 1796. It was the only press designed and constructed in Berks County; original in the museum of the *Reading Eagle*

grade. If we then finally look at firmness of principles, openness, straightforwardness, honesty and unselfishness, it becomes as clear as the light of day that Andrew Jackson should be preferred to John Qunicy Adams. If we consider the principles that should decide an election and the consequences thereof, it is impossible to grasp how a true patriot could hesitate to prefer General Jackson over Mister Adams" (Fig. 2.10).

This clear statement also influenced other German-American newspapers in Pennsylvania. Finally, 17 out of 27 German papers supported Jackson's candidacy.

One of the followers of Andrew Jackson was Henry A. Mühlenberg from Reading, who ran for the Senate. General Mühlenberg was a distinguished officer in the Revolutionary War and his daughter, Esther Mühlenberg, was married to Dr. Isaac Hiester, List's partner in his railway endeavor. Mühlenberg claimed that his successful election was mainly due to List's support.

During my visit to Reading, Peter Barbey drew my attention to the fact that, besides the *Readinger Adler*, broadsheets were published, i.e. one-pagers containing latest announcements. I wanted to know whether such broadsheets had been published when List was editor of the newspaper. With the help of the Historical Society of Reading, I was able to locate a broadsheet that constituted a kind of flyer in support of Jackson. It includes a direct comparison of Jackson and Adams, whereby Jackson is praised as an advocate of freedom and democracy while Adams is portrayed as an anti-democrat. An illustration showing Jackson as an 'upright'

American eagle and Adams as the bird standing on its head further documents the editor's opinion: The people should decide in favour of a strong and competent protector of democracy. Furthermore, a new electoral fraud should be avoided. With Adams freedom would be in jeopardy.

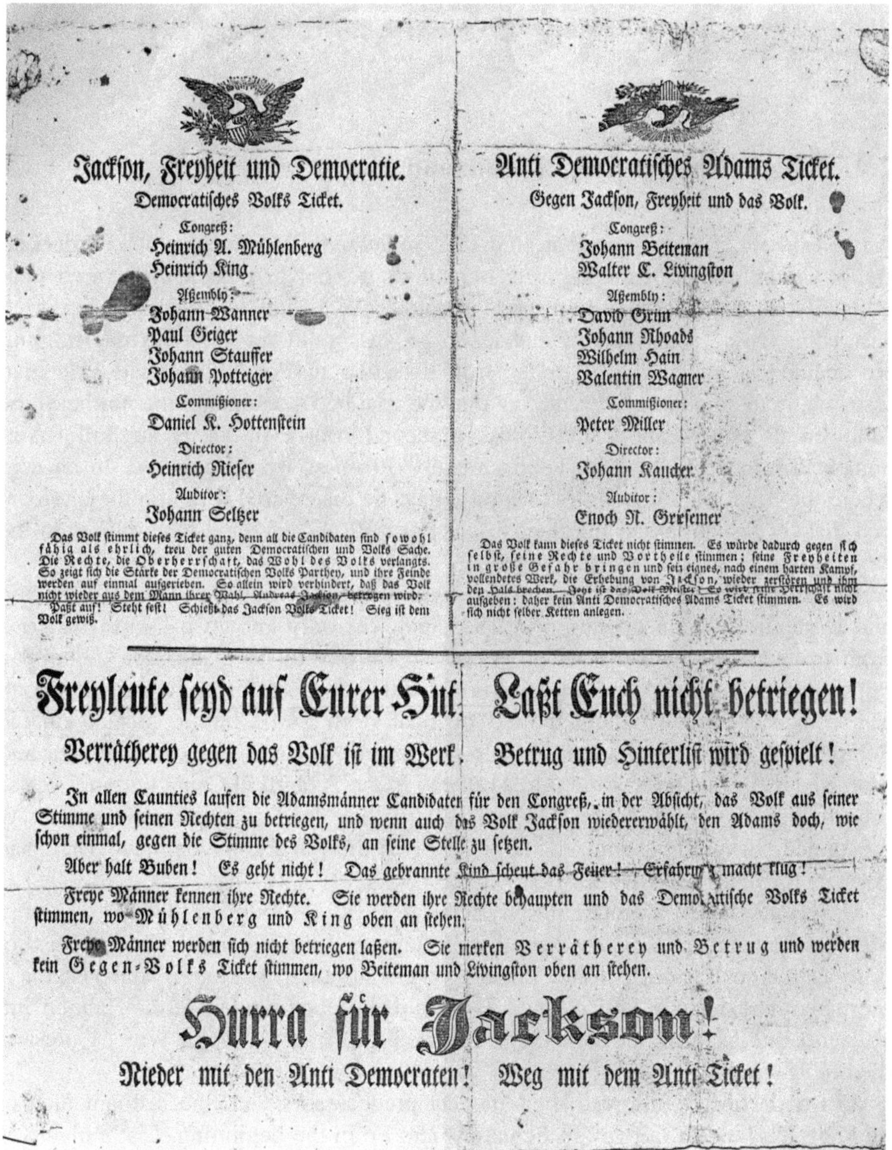

Jackson, Freyheit und Democratie.

Democratisches Volks Ticket.

Congreß:

Heinrich A. Mühlenberg

Heinrich King

Aßembly:

Johann Wanner

Paul Geiger

Johann Stauffer

Johann Potteiger

Commißioner:

Daniel K. Hottenstein

Director:

Heinrich Rieser

Auditor:

Johann Seltzer

Das Volk stimmt dieses Ticket ganz, denn all die Candidaten sind sowohl fähig als ehrlich, treu der guten Democratischen und Volks Sache. Die Rechte, die Oberherrschaft, das Wohl des Volks verlangts. So zeigt sich die Stärke der Democratischen Volks Parthey, und ihre Feinde werden auf einmal aufgerieben. So allein wird verhindert, daß das Volk nicht wieder aus dem Mann ihrer Wahl, Andreas Jackson, betrogen wird.

Paßt auf! Steht fest! Schießt das Jackson Volks Ticket! Sieg ist dem Volk gewiß.

Anti Democratisches Adams Ticket.

Gegen Jackson, Freyheit und das Volk.

Congreß:

Johann Beiteman

Walter C. Livingston

Aßembly:

David Grim

Johann Rhoads

Wilhelm Hain

Valentin Wagner

Commißioner:

Peter Miller

Director:

Johann Kaucher

Auditor:

Enoch R. Griesemer

Das Volk kann dieses Ticket nicht stimmen. Es würde dadurch gegen sich selbst, seine Rechte und Vortheile stimmen; seine Freyheiten in große Gefahr bringen und sein eignes, nach einem harten Kampf, vollendetes Werk, die Erhebung von Jackson, wieder zerstören und ihm den Hals brechen. Jetzt ist das Volk Meister! Es wird seine Herrschaft nicht aufgeben: daher kein Anti Democratisches Adams Ticket stimmen. Es wird sich nicht selber Ketten anlegen.

Freyleute seyd auf Eurer Hut! Laßt Euch nicht betriegen!

Verrätherey gegen das Volk ist im Werk. Betrug und Hinterlist wird gespielt!

In allen Caunties laufen die Adamsmänner Candidaten für den Congreß, in der Absicht, das Volk aus seiner Stimme und seinen Rechten zu betriegen, und wenn auch das Volk Jackson wiedererwählt, den Adams doch, wie schon einmal, gegen die Stimme des Volks, an seine Stelle zu setzen.

Aber halt Buben! Es geht nicht! Das gebrannte Kind scheut das Feuer! Erfahrung macht klug!

Freye Männer kennen ihre Rechte. Sie werden ihre Rechte behaupten und das Democratische Volks Ticket stimmen, wo Mühlenberg und King oben an stehen.

Freye Männer werden sich nicht betriegen laßen. Sie merken Verrätherey und Betrug und werden kein Gegen-Volks Ticket stimmen, wo Beiteman und Livingston oben an stehen.

Hurra für Jackson!

Nieder mit den Anti Democraten! Weg mit dem Anti Ticket!

Fig. 2.11 Broadsheet on the election campaign with a comparison of Andrew Jackson and John Quincy Adams; original in the Historical Society of Reading

The broadsheet also supports the candidacy of the Democrat H.A. Mühlenberg and closes with the exclamation: 'Hurray for Jackson! Down with the Anti-Democrat!'

The author of this enlightening document is unknown, but we must suppose that it was written by List. After all, it originated when List was in charge of the 'Readinger Adler'. The diction also matches. This type of political canvassing can still be found today, revealing how platitudes are used in dealing with political opponents (Fig. 2.11).

2.4 The Little Schuylkill Railroad

An investment boom occurred around 1825 in Schuylkill County, which borders on Berks County. Significant deposits of anthracite coal had been discovered near Pottsville, attracting tens of thousands of soldiers of fortune to the region. Friedrich List, being the quiet and attentive observer he was, could not resist the magical pull. He decided to travel the 70 miles from Reading to Pottsville and do his own research on the matter; after realizing that the coal bed stretched to the northeast, he followed its course and came across a second source of the Schuylkill River, namely the Little Schuylkill, approximately 30 miles from Pottsville. In an area where the town of Tamaqua is located today, he discovered a rich anthracite coal bed that by far surpassed the deposits of Pottsville. They were even closer to the next market in the city of Philadelphia.

If we consider that the first steam-driven railway of Europe between Stockton and Darlington began operation in 1825 and was only known in North America from hearsay, we realize how progressive List was to have the idea to build a railway from Tamaqua to Port Clinton, 22 miles away, in order to transport coal. The coal would then be transported by boat from Port Clinton, located on the Schuylkill Canal, to Phila-delphia. He contacted the landowners in this area and promised them that he would build a railway to the Schuylkill Canal within 5 years' time if they were willing to sell him half of their land at a favorable price. As mentioned earlier, List enlisted the support of the governor's nephew, Dr. Isaac Hiester, for his project (Fig. 2.12).

Dr. Isaac Hiester, a practicing physician in Reading, founded the Berks County Medical Society in 1824. He gave List's stepson, Karl Neidhard, his first insruc-tions in medical science. Later on, the boy continued his studies and became a prominent physician in Philadelphia. He was one of the founders of the Hahnemann Homeopathic Medical College there, founded the Brattleborough Water Cure and died in 1895 (5).

List and Hiester followed their modest predecessors with the brilliant idea of building the longest railway in Pennsylvania. From the beginning, List's plan was to move the wagons not with human labor or animals, but with a steam engine.

After the financing of the project had been clarified, the company began searching for a capable engineer who would be in charge of construction. List and

Fig. 2.12 Friedrich List discovering coal deposits in the Blue Mountains; drawing by A. v. Volborth; original in the possession of the author

Hiester found him and recruited Moncure Robinson, a young man of 27 years. The ground-breaking ceremony took place on June 1, 1829; on November 18, 1831 the stretch was completed—an incredible success, when we consider that the workers had to reclaim land seventeen times from a torrential river in order to construct the rail bed.

The railroad was officially opened on a Friday; the two horse-drawn cars, containing freight and approximately 60 persons each, had been built by Richard Imlay of Baltimore, Maryland. They left Port Clinton at 10 o'clock and arrived in Tamaqua at 1 o'clock p.m., where 15 cars were waiting, heavily laden with a most beautiful specimen of the Tamaqua coal (6) (Fig. 2.13).

Unfortunately the ceremonious inauguration of the Little Schuylkill Railway took place without its initiator and unflagging motor: List was returning from Europe at the time.

Fig. 2.13 Moncure Robinson (1801–1881); American civil engineer; original in the possession of the author

In his opening speech, Hiester commemorated List's pioneer work by saying: "In tendering my sincere acknowledgement for the flattering manner in which my name has been mentioned, I have to regret the absence on this joyous occasion, of one who is entitled to a full participation in the compliment with which I have been honored. The gentleman to whom I allude is Professor List, whose enterprise and public spirit are well known, and who is now on his homeward voyage from Europe, where he has, at his own expense, spent the last year, for the purpose of introducing the American anthracite. Associated as he was with me from the commencement, in designing and accomplishing the preliminary arrangements of the Little Schuylkill improvement, I take great pleasure in acknowledging how much the successful result of our labors is indebted to his talents, ingenuity and perseverance."

Dr. Isaac Hiester then offered a toast: "To Professor List—his efforts to introduce anthracite to the European markets deserve our thanks" (Fig. 2.14).

Six days later, on November 23rd, the first coal car was transported over the railroad to Port Clinton. Weighing three tons each, the first cars were driven by George Shoemaker and Henry Ray. Isaac Hinkley drove the first passenger coaches. Upon arrival at Port Clinton, the coal and passengers were transferred to barges for the trip to Philadelphia. During the first year of operation the coal-filled wagons were pulled by mules and horses. It was not until the winter 1833 that the locomotives "Comet" and "Catawissa", which the railroad company had ordered in England, finally arrived in Philadelphia (7).

Unfortunately they arrived when the Schuylkill Canal was frozen and the engines had to be hauled by horses to Port Clinton. When transported, the "Comet" and "Catawissa" were evidently taken off their wheels as an old cash book indicates separate charges for their transportation. These engines were of the 0-1-0 type and

Fig. 2.14 The original house of Moncure Robinson in Port Clinton, P.A.; photograph by E. Wendler, 2014

weighed less than eight tons. When acquired, the "Catawissa" was purchased for $5,000. It was first used on February 27, 1833 for a trial run not for public inspection. A newspaper correspondent mentioned that the engine left Tamaqua at ten o'clock and returned from Port Clinton in the evening. Of the six railroads in operation in Schuylkill County by the close of 1831, the Little Schuylkill was the first to install steam as a means of motive power (Fig. 2.15).

On March 9th, the engines were again placed in service for experimental trips. In the *Miner's Journal*, a weekly newspaper published in Pottsville, dated March 8, 1833, the public was invited to witness the trial runs. On the second trip, the "Catawissa" ran off a turnout and managed to pile up the thirteen cars it was hauling. All were more or less destroyed. Horses were dispatched to tow the engine to Tamaqua where repairs could be made. The "Comet" also ran off the track on its first trip. On March 11th the "Comet" left Tamaqua without a load for Port Clinton, where it met Thomas Sergeant, Edward Biddle, Moncure Robinson and some other officials who wanted to be transported to Tamaqua. The return trip from Port Clinton was made in two and a half hours. Both engines were placed in regular service on April 9, 1833, but horses still carried about one third of the tonnage on the road. The steam engine with 16 wagons travelled the stretch between Tamaqua and Port Clinton in two and one half hours, with each wagon carrying a load of 3

Fig. 2.15 The locomotive "Catawissa"; photograph by Smithsonian Institution, Chaney Collection, Washington, D.C.

tons. The train drove back and forth two times per day, so that approximately 100 tons of coal could be transported daily (8).

However, just two years later, another disaster struck when the "Catawissa" ran off the rails and into the river. It was towed to Tamaqua by a team of horses where it was repaired. The rail bed had first been plated with wooden rails that were fitted with iron. This construction was too weak, which could be the reason for the accident.

Nothing else is known about the "Comet" after August, 1833; the other engine, "Catawissa", had a long career. When the Little Schuylkill Railroad Company was leased by the Philadelphia Railroad Company in April 1863, this engine became a part of their locomotive fleet. Subsequently, the Pennsylvania Railroad Company rebuilt the "Catawissa" as a special inspection car to be used by their officers. It ran for a short time on the Lebanon Valley Branch between Reading and Harrisburg and apparently was not used after 1865. For the rest of its career, the" Catawissa" was stored at Reading until it was scrapped in 1870. This is the approximate date given by the railroad company; however, in the Philadelphia Railroad Company's Annual Report of 1871, the "Catawissa", along with another antiquated engine "Antilope", is recorded as having been sold for $4,000. It is unfortunate that the final location cannot be determined.

From the beginning, these engines attracted the attention of other railroads. Their profits and losses could show the stockholders the advantages of "steam locomotion" in comparison with horses (Fig. 2.16).

Fig. 2.16 The Little Schuylkill Railway with coal deposits; photograph by E. Wendler, 2014

2.5 Friedrich List—An Unknown Great American

In 1926 Harry Hickel published a speech held in Detroit under the title: "Friedrich List—An unknown great American". In his foreword, the author mentions the reasons for this small publication: "The presentation of this fragmentary record of List's achievements and experiences involves a two-fold purpose. Firstly, although List is as good as unknown to the present American generation, the intrinsic value of the man may impress itself on some occasional and sympathetic reader. Secondly, it is hoped that this bulletin, despite its obvious shortcoming, may be a conclusion of his historical importance for the United States. He was easily one of the most important politico-economical publicists in the United States during the first quarter of the nineteenth century. His influence and importance in the tariff controversies of that period, underestimated, if not almost wholly unknown and unrecognized, are nevertheless of inestimable significance" (9).

I found this unknown booklet in the archives of the Historical Society of Reading and believe that it deserves to be republished, especially since it confirms the knowledge that we already have of List's life and work:

2.5.1 A Discrete Thinker

A modest and unknown German landed in the US in the summer of 1825. This stranger quickly became acquainted with the foremost statesmen of the United States: he stood in intimate relationship with Henry Clay, James Madison, Andrew Jackson, Edward Livingston, Van Buren and Harrison and received written as well as spoken documentation of their appreciation.

The City of Philadelphia held a public banquet in his honor, after which he was given a set of resolutions publicly proclaiming the high regard in which that city held him.

How can we explain these attestations of esteem? His mission was not official; he came as a private citizen. Why did he attract so much attention from Americans who were in the highest circles of public and business life? Because he was a discrete thinker. His knowledge inevitably led him to fulfill an important mission here.

Let us recall that when he arrived in Philadelphia, the vast natural resources of the northern States were as yet untapped. Let us also recall that there were, as yet, no railroads (Fig. 2.17).

In 1825, the United States had been established some fifty years as a national political unity. This country was then taking its first unsteady, infantile steps in industry and commerce. It was emerging from its primitive, frontier, colonial wilderness status toward the unprecedented economic, agricultural, industrial giant is it today. These were the economic conditions of the age.

Simultaneously with these practical economic conditions, there then existed a theoretic treatise on public economy. This book was not only much in vogue at the time, but was regarded as an infallible authority in this field. Why it should be so much in vogue and regarded as incontestable authority is plain. It was the first publication on this subject. This book was popularly known as Adam Smith's 'Wealth of Nations', but had the fuller title: 'An Inquiry into the Nature and Causes of the Wealth of Nations'. It was the work of a Scotsman; Adam Smith had published it in 1776. Because of his book, Adam Smith is credited as being the founder of economics as a distinct field of human knowledge.

Fig. 2.17 The first steam engine passenger train in America; original in the Historical Museum in Port Clinton, P.A

Firstly, our Germanic newcomer was mentally equipped to understand thoroughly and to analyze scientifically and with exactitude, from the objects here to be practically observed, the then elemental constitution of the social fabric and the 1825 economic conditions of our country. Hamilton's famous 'Report on Manufactures', made to Congress as Secretary of the Treasury, made a deep impression on this German.

This man was Friedrich List. He had recently held the chair of professor of *Staatspraxis* and *Staatswissenschaft* at the University of Tübingen. For sheer merit, Friedrich List deserves to have his name as prominently and ineradicably blazoned on the political skies of both America and Germany, also on the roster of economic science, as does the name of that other renowned German, Franz Liszt, in the firmament of musical art.

Germans have ever played a great and indispensable part in the military victories, in the political events and the industrial development of the United States. So did the German, Friedrich List, play an important, indispensable, and today totally unknown and unrecognized part in America's development in the less spectacular politico-economic field. From his viewpoint as a talented political economist, Friedrich List at once recognized the practical requirements involved in America's national economic development. He became the mouthpiece for a new and influential economic trend and thereby clarified our national economic ideas. He firmly established the basis of our politico-economical needs and laid the basis for a new and definite direction to our national policies. He made clear the relationship of economic activity to political power.

Here he continued a thorough historical study of nations and of peoples. These studies, completed in America, led him to active and lively opposition to the tenets of Adam Smith. List, at first, had believed in the infallibility of Smith's theories. However, he did not long permit himself to be thus deluded. The 'cosmopolitical economy' and 'philanthropic' views of Smith were abandoned by List in the light of his practical American observations; also because of the great changes going on in Europe. List showed Smith's position, in the main, to be based on dogmatic economic doctrines. This came as a shock to many of Smith's followers, many of whom had, and still persisted in looking upon the principles of Adam Smith as incontrovertible. List, in America, opposed Adam Smith's cosmopolitan or universal economy with his own conclusion designated as 'national economy'; he also established a distinction between Smith's 'cosmopolitan' and his own ideas of 'political economy'.

Again and again, List emphasized the main distinction between his 'national' idea and that of Adam Smith's 'cosmopolitan' school. List's teaching embraced the idea of nationality: that the nation is the link between the individual and mankind. In the words of Arthur Griffith, the first Prime Minister of the Republic of Ireland, who was a great follower of List's economic ideas: 'In the economy of Adam Smith there was no place for the soul of a nation. To him the associations of the past possessed no value. In the economy of List, the nation not only possessed a place, but the highest place.'

List not only showed that the theories of Adam Smith were not infallible maxims and incapable of universal applications, but that, on the contrary, Smith's doctrines were admirably adapted to foster and securely establish the economic prosperity of one nation alone: England. When applied to another nation they might be ruinous. In

Fig. 2.18 The Ohio-Pennsylvania Railroad about 1840; original in the possession of the author

opposition, he offered his 'American System'. Eventually, List believed that Adam Smith had introduced a spirit of sophistry, confusion and hypocrisy into political economy: he exposed what he thought was Smith's unsound or weak logic and sophistical arguments. Adam Smith stood for universal, cosmopolitan, free trade. This policy was all right for England's welfare. But herein England played the part of the double dealer. List noted that while English statesmen and parliamentarians mouthed great catchwords like Adam Smith's 'freedom', their practical conduct was just the opposite. They supposed freedom only served the purpose of making other nations the economic subjects of the British lion. Through Smith's school, England seductively preached free trade principles to the world and persuaded other nations to buy English manufactured articles; she, however, put forth restrictive regulations and repressive policies against these foreign countries and had no desire to buy their products. List early sensed the malignant influence of England's insular supremacy. He showed Americans at a crucial moment that the national economies of America and England were, and must be, thoroughly dissimilar.

Smith contended that the wealth of nations consisted in the abundance of their 'exchange values', that is, in their possession of commodities. These commodities or 'values', in order to be exchanged, had to be carried in ships: this meant foreign commerce. List incidentally detected that this foreign commerce meant an exchange on such a basis that there always remained a trade balance in England's favor. List opposed Smith's 'exchange value theory' with his assertion that the wealth of a nation did not consist in the quantity of the 'exchange value' it possesses, but in the active, full and many-sided development of its 'productive powers'.

Was List's political economy, similar to most political economies, mere pedantic speculation and dry theorizing? By no means, it was based on observation (Fig. 2.18).

List, on arrival in the United States, observed the very beginnings of the evolution of the American economy. To repeat: 'The best book on political economy which one can read in America is life itself.' Continuing, he said: 'Here before one's eyes the vast expanses of wilderness become rich and powerful states. Here it first became clear to me that nations pass through different stages of economic development. A process, which in Europe would require many centuries, takes place here under my very eyes—I mean the transition from a state of nature to pastoral cultivation, from that to agriculture, and from that to manufacture and commerce. Here we can observe how rent gradually grows from zero to an important sum. Here a simple farmer by practical experience has a better understanding of the means by which agriculture and rent can be advanced than the keenest intellects of the old world—he tries to attract manufacturers and artificers into the vicinity. Here the contrast between agricultural and manufacturing nations shows itself in the clearest manner and causes the most violent agitations. Nowhere so well as here, can we learn the true value of means of transport and its influence on the intellectual and material life of the people. I read this book with eagerness and industry, and thought to bring the lessons I learned from it into harmony with my former studies, experience and reflections.'

Remarkable as it was to see all these changes so clearly, what made List so conspicuous a figure in America was his exceptional talent in applying to various stages of economic development, from an agricultural to an industrial society, the indispensable economic principles; moreover, in proposing the political action which this evolution demanded in order that the nation, through added welfare and greater prosperity, might be the gainer therefrom. Out of this arose List's idea of industrial politics. It is the economic task of the state, he urged, to bring into existence through legislative and administration action, the conditions required for the progress of the nation. List argued, in effect: open up a new railroad and the national wealth is not increased by finding bulk silver or gold nuggets along the way. Its construction involves the consumption of food, iron, stone, wood, of man and animal power. The state has these commodities in superabundance. In converting this material, muscular and mental superabundance into railroads, lasting and permanent values were created; furthermore, an instrument was created which doubled the productive powers of a nation. More striking, however, than this was the fact that List early and clearly saw something that transcended the influence of the railroads: the extension of markets and lowering of prices. The railroad would be something more than a transporting and distributing system. He said: 'Here, in the United States, I began to consider it from the standpoint of the theory of productive powers, and in its combined operation as a national transport system, consequently in its influence on the whole intellectual and political life, social intercourse, productive powers, and material strength of the country.'

According to List: 'Developing a country's resources makes it independent.' This development is conditioned on protection, so that, protected from competition with stronger rivals, the nation's new or 'infant' industries can expand. After they are sufficiently strong, protection should be withdrawn and competition returns as a healthy stimulant. Hamilton's protective views were improved upon. Whereas Hamilton founded his arguments on expediency, List based his protective views on his theory of nationality. For any man to have made acceptable emendations to a policy of Hamilton's, was, in itself, an outstanding achievement. Alexander Hamilton is the foremost American statesman of all time. Having transcended

American confines, Hamilton has been judged by a universally famed contemporary as one of the three greatest men in the world of his time.

Of these chosen three, Hamilton was placed as ranking best. The judgment was pronounced by that competent analyzer of men's capacities: Napoleon.

It had been some years since we had ceased to be British colonies and had gotten away from the coercion of being compelled to buy manufactured goods from England. It was the oppressive policy of English statesmen, voiced by Lord Chatham, that even a horseshoe nail should not be permitted to be made here. Ostensibly, that economic slavery was over with. But for a time, necessity drove the young republic to continue in the same commercial path. During that period our forefathers were still almost exclusively engaged in agriculture. In 1826 the change was setting in, as List observed. Industry in its infancy was springing up. America was developing more and more, through a steady increase in the number of factories, into a commercial nation which could now begin to contend seriously with England's supremacy. America's commercial conflict with England was leading to mutual retaliations.

În about 1826, America was about to part ways economically with England. This crisis was as important and as far reaching, if not as spectacular, as the severance of political ties through the war of 1776. In that declaration of America's industrial, commercial and economic independence from England, the German, Friedrich List, played a leading, if not the most important, part.

The 'Pennsylvania Society for the Promotion of Manufacturers and the Mechanic Arts' (founded by Hamilton) was an active agency on behalf of protection. Its Vice-President, Charles Ingersoll, was a leading citizen of Philadelphia. He had made the acquaintance of List and was deeply impressed by List's ability. Ingersoll and his influential associates, as well as America's statesmen, appreciated the value of List's scholarly, sound opposition to the predominant system of Adam Smith. A national convention of protectionists, to be held at Harrisburg, was called by Ingersoll to formulate proposals for a new tariff. List entered the controversy as a fully equipped champion and delivered a lecture which scientifically justified America's protection tariff policy. Speaking in the state capitol's House of Representatives, he shattered the arguments of Prof. Thomas Cooper, President of South Carolina College, the leading American advocate of free trade. Later on List stated that this convention proclaimed, in the name of the people, the Economic Declaration of Independence of the United States. List's speech was printed in the *Philadelphia National Journal* and in fifty additional newspapers throughout the United States. Reproduced as a pamphlet, List's exposition, among other things, had the effect of influencing the report of the Secretary of the Treasury, Richard Rush, to Congress. The pamphlet, in fact, was so successful that, in recognition of his services, List was tendered a complimentary dinner at the Mansion House in Philadelphia. This was November 3, 1827. It is recorded that List, although speaking a language foreign to him, delivered a remarkable piece of eloquent as well as scholarly treatise. The cordiality shown List that evening ran so high that some wit proposed the toast: 'May this society be never List-less of their true interests.' List was no mere academic pedant; along with his gift for analysis of politico-economic problems, he brought to his cause a fluent and a clear pen, a contagious enthusiasm and a fervency of delivery. He was, in fact, a high class publicist.

A few days later, as further appreciation of the unrivalled aid List rendered, the following set of resolutions was passed: ‘Whereas it has appeared to the society that great and important interests of the United States have suffered and are suffering much for want of sufficient dissemination of the true principles of political economy; and whereas the enemies of the American system are ceaseless in their exertions to cause to be republished and disseminated in large numbers the inapposite maxims of Smith, Say and other writers, which, however sound they may be as abstract principles in cosmopolitan economy, experience has fully proven them inapplicable to the present state of the commercial world. And whereas Professor Friedrich List has proven himself a man of profound knowledge in the science of political economy, and has opened new and fundamental principles, clearing away the errors and removing the prejudices which have hitherto made a mystery of that science, and has thereby rendered it plain and comprehensible to every capacity; and whereas this society is very desirous that Professor List should proceed forthwith to publish and disseminate his new and fundamental views of that important science for the use of schools, and so in a full and extended treatise, it is therefore, resolved, that this society does earnestly call on Professor List to prepare and publish as soon as may be, an elementary work for the use of schools, and also an elaborate treatise on political economy adapted particularly to the situation in the United States (Fig. 2.19).

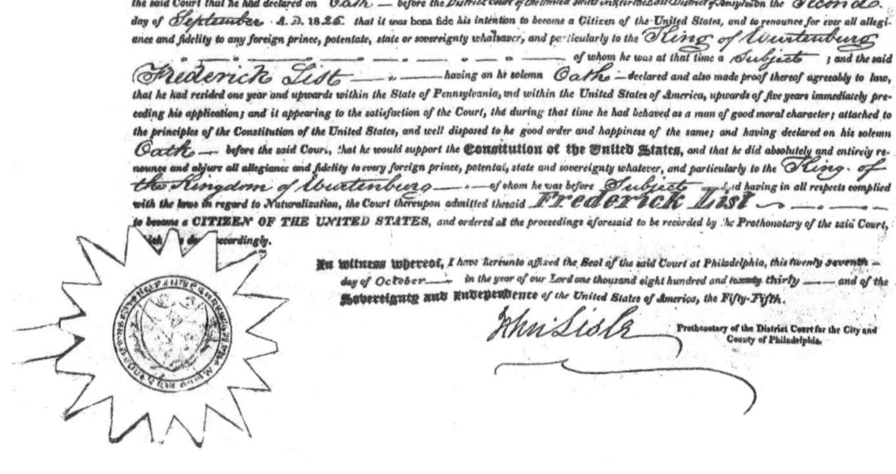

Be it remembered, THAT at the District Court for the City and County of Philadelphia, held at the City of Philadelphia, in the Commonwealth of Pennsylvania, in the United States of America, on the Second day of October in the year of our Lord one thousand eight hundred and Thirty Frederick List a native of Reuttingen in Wurtenburg exhibited a petition, praying to be admitted to become a CITIZEN OF THE UNITED STATES, and it appearing to the said Court that he had declared on Oath before the District Court of the United States in & for the East. District of Pensylvania on the Second day of September A. D. 1826 that it was bona fide his intention to become a Citizen of the United States, and to renounce for ever all allegiance and fidelity to any foreign prince, potentate, state or sovereignty whatsoever, and particularly to the King of Wurtenburg of whom he was at that time a Subject; and the said Frederick List having on his solemn Oath declared and also made proof thereof agreeably to law, that he had resided one year and upwards within the State of Pennsylvania, and within the United States of America, upwards of five years immediately preceding his application; and it appearing to the satisfaction of the Court, that during that time he had behaved as a man of good moral character; attached to the principles of the Constitution of the United States, and well disposed to the good order and happiness of the same; and having declared on his solemn Oath before the said Court, that he would support the Constitution of the United States, and that he did absolutely and entirely renounce and abjure all allegiance and fidelity to every foreign prince, potentate, state and sovereignty whatever, and particularly to the King of the Kingdom of Wurtenburg of whom he was before Subject and having in all respects complied with the laws in regard to Naturalization, the Court thereupon admitted the said Frederick List to become a CITIZEN OF THE UNITED STATES, and ordered all the proceedings aforesaid to be recorded by the Prothonotary of the said Court, which was done accordingly.

In witness whereof, I have hereunto affixed the Seal of the said Court at Philadelphia, this twenty seventh day of October in the year of our Lord one thousand eight hundred and twenty thirty and of the Sovereignty and Independence of the United States of America, the Fifty-Fifth.

John Lisle
Prothonotary of the District Court for the City and County of Philadelphia.

Fig. 2.19 On October 27, 1830 the naturalization papers were signed and sealed, making Friedrich (Frederick) List a US citizen

Furthermore it is resolved, that this society does recommend the said Professor List to the members of the Congress of the United States, the legislature of the State of Pennsylvania and other legislature bodies, the several universities and public seminaries of learning, and to their fellow-countrymen generally for their aid in enabling him to accomplish this desirable object.

Furthermore it is resolved, that this society will subscribe for fifty copies of each work and will do all in their power, individually and collectively, to procure subscribers, and in every way to aid Professor List in his laudable undertaking.'

As has ever been historically the case, here in America, southerners showed themselves to be the German's critics and enemies.

George Mc Duffie (1790–1851), Governor from South Carolina, after reading a passage from the address to Congress presented by the Harrisburg Convention, ridiculed its style:

'The Harrisburg Convention stands much more in need of a Professor of Rhetoric than they do of a Professor of Political Economy'. 'There is', the polemical and bombastic McDuffie tells us, 'a certain German Professor of Political Economy and Necromancy in Pennsylvania, who has recently been introduced to the American public by a member of the Harrisburg Convention. I must do him the justice to say that no one could have been selected of more eminent qualifications to lecture from the text of the Harrisburg Address. Professor List is no doubt a legitimate descendent of the Rosicrucians who once figured in Germany; and I cannot but congratulate the Harrisburg Convention in having supplied the desideratum which they so much lamented by a professor of political economy who bids so fair to be the discoverer of this philosopher's stone.'

The next day his equally bombastic colleague Hamilton, carrying on the sarcasm, remarked on the floor of Congress that 'we appear to have imported a professor from Germany, in absolute violation of the doctrines of the American System, to lecture upon its lessons—to convince Adam Smith of stupidity and Ricardo of error.'

Friedrich List was a pioneer in advocating America's present protective tariff policy. He was easily one of the most important politico-economical publicists in the United States during the first quarter of the nineteenth century. His influence and importance in the tariff controversies of that period, underestimated if not almost wholly unknown and unrecognized, are nevertheless of inestimable importance.

2.5.2 *The Tragedy of List's Career*

When List landed in the US, he came upon invitation of Lafayette, whom he joined in Albany, while the latter made his 'triumphal' tour of our country. In Boston on the 50th anniversary of the Battle of Bunker Hill, List witnessed the laying of the cornerstone of the Bunker Hill Monument. It was doubtless through Lafayette's friendship and prestige that List became so readily acquainted with our leading men. List eventually quit Lafayette's somewhat theatrical procession and bought a ten-acre farm with a house near Harrisburg. Thither he moved his family. The undertaking was a failure. List's zeal stood him in poor stead as a practical farmer. The guileless national economist was unmercifully swindled by the wily Yankee seller. In addition, his new Yankee neighbors took mean advantage of the inexperienced German professor. The property had many drawbacks not apparent to List at the time of purchase. The house was damp, the winter severe, the children came down with fever in the summer, his family suffered. The place had to be abandoned; it was to be disposed of at a sacrifice sale. No buyers were found.

List thereupon gladly seized the offer to take over the editorship of the *Adler* popularly known as the 'Berks County Bible'. It had a large circulation (3,600), and, as its German readers accepted its assertions with full faith, the paper yielded a great influence. During his four years' incumbency of the editorship, List's Philadelphia triumphs followed. It seems, however, that the lure of the hinterland again diverted List and drew him from these triumphs to the Blue Mountains of Pennsylvania. This excursion was fraught with practical results. Here List accidentally discovered a tract of land very rich in anthracite coal. With his exceptional insight, List recognized the significance of his find. To increase the value of this product by means of transportation was from then on List's main thought. His literary work and publicity efforts had to be abandoned. List thereupon had the achievement of having organized a company of capitalists within a very short period and raised the sum, remarkably large for conditions of 100 years ago, of $1,000,000. List then planned and began building one of America's first railways. It ran from Tamaqua to Port Clinton on the Little Schuylkill River. Completed and officially opened in 1831, this new railroad with river transport conception opened America's anthracite coal fields to the European market. The two towns at the terminals were new creations. Tamaqua today is a city of 12,000. Later on, List's railroad was destined to develop into an important link of one of America's greatest 'coal carrier' railroads, the Philadelphia & Reading.

The coal mine also was financially successful. List was assured of a substantial portion of the profits. Managed, as time went on, by the Lehigh Coal & Navigation Company and the Philadelphia & Treading Coal & Iron Company, it produced an excellent quality of anthracite.

2.5.3 The Prophet Is Never with Honor in His Own Land

After finally having had some financial success, List could now devote himself to the great projects his energetic and resourceful mentality incessantly planned.

Where was his mind dwelling? Previous to coming here, sordid, systematic and unremitting persecution by narrow-minded Württemberg bureaucrats had been so continuous that List was harassed to the point of quitting Germany altogether. List, as Deputy from Reutlingen, had proposed some reforms to the Württemberg Chamber, coupled with criticism of the administrative, judicial and financial regime of the state. For this, List was accused, tried, found guilty of sedition and condemned to ten month's imprisonment, release, rearrest, then his final determination to leave all behind and go to the United States to join Lafayette, whom he had met in Paris in 1823 and who had urged List to take the American trip with him.

In Württemberg, List had been hounded. Wherever else he sought refuge, there followed pernicious hints of the vindictive Württemberg authorities and life was made unendurable for him. Here in America, on the contrary, he had connections with America's greatest men; riches had come to him. He was living happily with his wife and children: he found sympathetic cooperation, teamwork and an unlimited outlet for his peculiar talent, aspiring initiative, inexhaustible capacity and fiery energy. So, what seemed more logical than that the scene of his next big operations should be staged in the United States? Logical, yes. But List's loyalty towards his "Heimat" led him to cast common sense aside. Although his activities and his successes were here, his thoughts returned ever to Germany. He had a practical mind and it found expression here, but 'das deutsche Herz' longed for the fatherland. In fact, in the midst of all his rousing activities here, List genuinely felt 'Heimweh' for Germany. For all his American glory and established fortune, he was unhappy. On October 5, 1828, in Philadelphia, he fell to reading some Hamburg newspapers. Indescribable feelings overpowered him. Six weeks of steady 'Heimweh', in fact, made him useless for the pursuit of his business enterprises. Up there in Pennsylvania's Blue Ridge Mountains he dreamed of a German national railway system that was still to be. 'In the background of all my plans', he said, 'lies Germany, the return to Germany'. There is something tragic in this unconquerable longing for the fatherland. The sentiment allured him. Selfish motives, self-interest never seem to have actuated the man at any time throughout his life (Fig. 2.20).

The fatal attraction proved irresistible and he returned to Europe. Through President Andrew Jackson, List was appointed to the American Consulate of Hamburg. This appointment was an expression of Jackson's appreciation towards List and the German community that supported him in the election. It was an evenly balanced election, and the throwing of the united mass of German votes on behalf of 'Old Hickory' helped decide the election in his favor. During a visit at the White House, List was assured of Jackson's appreciation for the steadfast devotion shown by Pennsylvania Germans for the President.

But the Hamburg government, infected by obdurate Württemberg, objected on the grounds that List was 'a dangerous political fugitive'. After a brief stay in Europe, during which he scouted out his future options there, he returned to the United States to get his family. While here, he was promised the United States Consularship at Leipzig. It was an unsalaried position, but on his arrival in Leipzig, from that vantage point, he launched the movement of the German national railway system. Due to List's efforts, the first railway linking Dresden and Leipzig was finally completed. In the midst of List's bitter struggles, America suffered a depression and his Pennsylvania coal mine ceased to yield revenue.

Again, this man who so thoroughly knew that the economy was indispensable to the prosperity of nations, who devoted his energies to the development of the wealth of two nations, in particular, Germany and the United States, this man in the midst of his manifold and unselfish endeavors made a mess of his own personal

Fig. 2.20 List as economics and transportation consultant; drawing by Hans Baluschek; original in the possession of the author

affairs and prosperity, and seemingly pauperized himself. When List was in Belgium, just after it was created an independent state, conditions there engrossed his entire attention. Inclinations toward his fatherland, combined with love for the United States, led him to recognize the importance of a new avenue of commerce for intercourse between America and Germany. His pet idea was that Antwerpen should be joined to the River Rhine by means of a railroad and so bring the new, young, independent kingdom in closest contact with Germany, thus opening up new sources of national prosperity for both.

List was well aware of the causes underlying Germany's economic poverty and political bankruptcy. The multitude of petty German states had effectively divided and hopelessly weakened his country. This anachronistic condition, leading to conflicting, warring, intranational rivalries, was clearly traceable to the leftover heritage of the Middle Ages. The condition of standing still had too long persisted. Germany needed to adjust to the evolution very apparent in the internal organization of Germany's neighbors and contemporaries. The state of Prussia alone then had within its boundaries sixty-seven different tariffs.

The famous "Zollverein" (Tarrif Union) was established as the result of List's untiring zeal. Through the Tarrif Union the German people were emancipated from the galling fetters of innumerable tariff restrictions and internal customs barriers. This excellent innovation was the institution which evidenced the first pronounced step toward German unification and nationality. Due to List, a practical as well as a political consciousness was aroused in Germany after centuries of slumber. Amidst a sea of troubles, amidst animosities growing more bitter and relentless, amidst continuing persecutions, List contrived not only additional means for bringing about German national unity, but guarantees to insure the permanence of that nationality were planned by him. These were a German postal system, railroad extensions, and the relegation of government by bureaucracy.

The prophet is never with honor in his own land. It must have been soothing to List to have received, during his lifetime, a glowing tribute from a foreign country. From France, in the year 1845, Richelot, French translator of the *National System*, said: 'In Germany there lives a man who without office, without title, without riches has become, principally through his patriotism and talent, a mighty power. In France we certainly know this regal rule of intelligence which sways a pen as its scepter, but in Germany this is an extraordinary manifestation. Dr. List is the moral founder of the German Zollverein and of the German railways. These two, the greatest achievements in Germany of a quarter of a century, evolved from his brain' (Fig. 2.21).

This unusual career was the only one of its kind to be recorded in Germany. To Richelot's excellent summary, he might have added that without academic or official backing, with no other advantage than the inexhaustibility of his spiritual resources, an iron will and fluent pen, it was possible for List to rise as a private

Fig. 2.21 Friedrich Lis, lithography of J. Kriehuber; original in the possession of the author

citizen from the ranks of the common people to a self-created position of influence, even of independent power. Although isolated and working single-handedly, without a newspaper, without a political party, without the resolution of legitimate meetings, he evolved into such a power in Europe that he brought bureaus, offices and counting-rooms into a furor, made ministries uncomfortable and was the center of an exchange of voluminous diplomatic correspondence. During five and one-half years in America, the political fugitive became a conspicuous public figure, orator, journalist, politician, promoter of an extensive coal mine, builder of one of the first railways and ended up as a Yankee Consul.

List's agitation seems to have had far reaching results at all times. Just as he had influenced the report of our Secretary of the Treasury, there is no doubt that when Bismarck broke with free-trade, and in that breach furnished the protection policy with some of its most effective arguments, his action was ascribable to the conscious or unconscious influence of List.

Conclusion

List's aggressive manner in public originated in the vivaciousness and earnestness of his convictions. His personal qualities were quite the contrary. His was a mild, kindly nature, dominated by unsuspecting sacrifice, devotion to his friends and love for his family. List was upright, confiding, jovial and hearty. An inexhaustible happiness was combined with roughish Swabian humor. He was good-natured and benevolent. In his conflicts with opponents, he never had the person, only the issue in mind. The brisk, refreshing and agile nature of his spirit made personal contact and conversation with him exceedingly magnetic. Ever new and original, bubbling over with creative ideas and projects, he acted as a stimulus and exercised an awakening, inciting and fructifying influence upon all who came in contact with him. As it is reported of an ancient orator, so did List invariably leave the soul of another impregnated with an edifying spur. This lively, rousing, fervent power was noticeable also in his gift of presentation. List was imbued with an intense and passionate patriotism. It is reported that he had a titanic head (Fig. A.1).

In List's numerous articles, reports Heinrich Laube, 'there was more than mere knowledge and actual proofs; there was urgent and compelling life in these articles; a complete, powerful man ordered, ruled, drove and subjugated us behind these lines and sentences, which ever ascended and expanded in artistic merit and before reaching the highest culmination of expression. Those whom they did not convince, they captivated. A genius battled in List's words. Nothing was dry in his treatise.' (Fig. A.2).

E. Wendler, *Friedrich List's Exile in the United States*,
SpringerBriefs in Economics, DOI 10.1007/978-3-319-23642-1

Fig. A.1 List-Bust of the American sculptor Angelo DiMaria of Reading, 1996

Fig. A.2 Vignette with an allegory of the god Hermes; the patron saint of merchants; in: Otto, F.: Das Buch berühmter Kaufleute, Leipzig und Berlin 1868, p. 93

References

Wendler, E.: Friedrich List (1789–1846), A Visionary Economist with Social Responsibility; Heidelberg 2014.
Wendler, E.: Friedrich List (1789–1846), An Historical Figure and Pioneer in German-American Relations; Gräfelfing 1989.
N.N.: Reading-Reutlingen, August 1989; in: Historical Review of Berks County, Fall 1989, p. 156 f. and 196 f.
Society Awarded List Prize in Germany; in: Historical Review of Berks County, Winter 1996/67; p. 4–67.
Klamkin, M.: The Return of Lafayette (1824–25); New York 1975.
Altner, H. G.: Friedrich List (1789–1846); in: Historical Review of Berks County, October 1935, p. 7–11.
Hart, G. M.: The Comet and Catawissa – Two Historic Engines for Little Schuylkill R.R.; in: Railway & Locomotive Bulletin 46; p. 32 f.
Serfass, D.R.: Iron Steps, Illustrated History of Tamaqua, P.A., 1995; p. 1–6.
Hickel, H.: Friedrich List (1789–1846), Detroit 1926.

E. Wendler, *Friedrich List's Exile in the United States*,
SpringerBriefs in Economics, DOI 10.1007/978-3-319-23642-1

MIX
Papier aus verantwortungsvollen Quellen
Paper from responsible sources
FSC® C105338

If you have any concerns about our products,
you can contact us on
ProductSafety@springernature.com

In case Publisher is established outside the EU,
the EU authorized representative is:
Springer Nature Customer Service Center GmbH
Europaplatz 3, 69115 Heidelberg, Germany

Printed by Libri Plureos GmbH
in Hamburg, Germany